365
Daily Advocacy Tips

365
Daily Advocacy Tips

Leslie Cuthbert
Solicitor Advocate, Consultant and Trainer

Bloomsbury Professional

Bloomsbury Professional, Maxwelton House, 41–43 Boltro Road, Haywards Heath, West Sussex, RH16 1BJ

© Bloomsbury Professional 2015

Reprinted 2015

Bloomsbury Professional is an imprint of Bloomsbury Publishing Plc

British Library Cataloguing-in-Publication Data.

A catalogue record for this book is available from the British Library.

ISBN 978 1 78043 832 0

Typeset by Phoenix, Chatham, Kent

Printed and bound in Great Britain by CPI Group (UK) Ltd, Croydon, CR0 4YY

Foreword

This book is a good idea.

Improvement in the courtroom will be swift if an advocate holds a crisp new thought daily.

The ideas here will help you.

Make a habit of each morning of opening these pages.

What I like is there will be one idea every day – and only one. Your mind will not get jumbled. Think on what you read. Try and apply that idea straightaway to a case that very morning, whether in court or during preparation of papers.

Some ideas you will like. Others may not work for you. With advocacy, this is always the way. But the point is to try things out – one day at a time.

Iain Morley QC

Author
'The Devil's Advocate'

Preface

'I can't teach anybody anything, all I can do is make them think' – Socrates

This book is not specific to one geographical area nor is it related to one specific area of law. It is designed to have points that will be of interest and assistance to anyone engaged in advocacy – oral or written – in any forum. Similarly it can be read from first page to last or alternatively you may dip in and out jumping between tips as you wish. I also hope that this will be a text you will benefit from returning to again and again.

You may well think to yourself as you read one tip or another, 'I'd never say/do that before Judge X' and I'm sure that your judgement would be correct. This book isn't designed to necessarily teach you anything but rather, as the quote above illustrates, to make you think and help you to evolve your own style of advocacy. Some points you may be familiar with, some I am certain you won't be, but even where you may initially disagree with a point be careful that your response isn't solely due to 'cognitive dissonance' (and if you don't know what that is you might like to start by going to Tip 117).

There are various themes in this book and some of the tips provided have more than one application, or can be placed under different headings. To help you identify particular areas of interest the Contents list (p xi) gives you an indication of which theme a tip primarily falls under. However, you will undoubtedly conclude that some tips are relevant to another topic and some entries will specifically cross-reference other tips.

To keep up-to-date on further assorted tips you may wish to choose to follow 'consultingadvocate' on Twitter.

Leslie Cuthbert
February 2015

Acknowledgements

My advocacy journey began not at law school but after unflinching advice from one man, my good friend and an amazing advocate, Iain Morley QC. I'd also like to express my gratitude to all the advocacy trainers and students I've worked with. I have learnt invaluable lessons from every one of them but most of all from my pal from across the pond Charles Dewey Cole Jr.

A number of friends and colleagues from all spheres of the legal profession have been kind enough to read this tome in draft and have given their comments on it and I truly appreciate their efforts. Thank you therefore to my great ami John Lane, to whom I owe so much, to the tenacious and talented Kelly Thomas, to the cultured and erudite Kenneth Dow and to the judicious and insightful Annabel Pilling.

I am also grateful to Kiran Goss and everyone at Bloomsbury Professional for being willing to take this project, and myself, on.

Contents

PREPARATION

Effective trial advocacy relies on preparation which begins as soon as you are instructed as the trial advocate. Your aim should be to read the papers a minimum of three times before the trial.

Use the 1st read through of the papers to identify the legal framework ie who bears the burden of proving what and what is the standard of proof which the decision maker will apply. In addition identify the issues which are in dispute.

The 2nd read through of the papers should be used to analyse the facts, dividing them into good facts (ie those that help your client or argument), bad facts (ie those that harm your client/argument), fixed facts (ie those which are incapable of being altered) and changeable facts (ie those which, as a result of further evidence or cross-examination, may be capable of being altered). Once you have carried out the fact analysis you ought then to go on to create a case theory, this being the essence of the closing speech you would wish to give if all goes according to plan in your trial.

Finally for the 2nd read through you ought to then reduce your case theory down into a case theme. This is a short headline, similar to the headline you'd find in a newspaper, that summarises your overall case strategy in one sentence, eg:

> 'There was never a contract because there was never an agreement.'

> 'This is a case of mistaken identity due to the poor lighting and distance.'

Finally the 3rd read through should be done just before the trial, after any further evidence has arrived. This should be used specifically to plan how you intend to cross-examine each witness to change bad facts to good facts and to have sufficient facts for your closing speech.

Dopamine and epinephrine are hormones and neuro transmitters that help mental alertness. Both come from an amino acid found in proteins. Accordingly before you are going to have to make a speech you may find that you benefit from eating protein.

If you're feeling nervous focus on your breathing. The reason being that by slowing your breathing, and taking bigger breaths as opposed to fast, shallow breaths, you can help control the production of adrenaline/cortisol in your body. If adrenaline reduces in production then your nerves should lessen to a degree as well. Advocates therefore may benefit from having an awareness of 'mindfulness'.

An overlooked aspect of preparing for trial is getting enough sleep.

Various research studies into sleep have demonstrated that if you sleep for less than seven hours a night there is an enormous impact upon your ability to remain attentive.

What's worse is that this effect can be cumulative so that if you regularly deprive yourself of sleep (as many advocates often do) your ability to focus and maintain attention deteriorates further.

Ensure you dress appropriately and professionally. Image and body language are crucially important as the majority of the initial impact we have is based upon how we look.

If you don't believe this bear in mind that one judge's motto is:

> 'The burden of proof rests on the lawyer in the polyester suit.'

Be in control of the documents. An advocate's presentation and confidence can easily be undermined if they are seen to be scrabbling around seeking a particular item.

Tabs, colour coding, separate folders – whatever you need to do to marshal the papers do it!

It is a mistake ever to deliver an opening speech
without a plan. It is not necessary to have written out
every word but you ought to have at least an outline.

Focus on having good posture. Despite what you
might sometimes see in television programmes the
'slouching' advocate approach is rarely very effective.

Be sure you know how to use whatever technology
you're going to need in court as fumbling with
electronic devices may make you look amateurish and,
as a result, undermine your credibility.

Type out your notes for cross-examination – complete with headings and sub-headings – as this will be an aid in ensuring your examination has a structure and it allows you to re-visit issues.

Also typing them out means you won't be trying to deduce from your handwriting what a particular word is!

Preparing for an expert's cross-examination should include a reading of the expert's website, if they have one, as this will often turn up points you can use during your cross-examination of them.

Being able to 'think on your feet' is often said to be a skill which many advocates wish that they had or want to develop.

However, as Howard L Nations said, it all comes back to thorough preparation:

> 'Extemporaneous brilliance on cross-examination increases in direct proportion to extreme diligence in planning and preparation.'

When drafting think of the Henry Kissinger story and ask yourself, 'Is this the best I can do?'

The story goes as follows:

It's 1971 and Henry Kissinger calls in one of his aides, Winston Lord, and asks for a status report on the Allende regime in Chile. This is a great opportunity for the aide who talks to some people, makes some phone calls and turns in a ten-page document at the end of the week.

On Monday morning, Kissinger calls the aide into his office. They sit in silence for a moment then Kissinger picks up the document and drops it saying, 'Is this the best you can do?' The aide replies, 'No, no. You said it was a rush job, and I ... let me have it.'

The aide goes away, looks up some local Chilean newspapers, adds some maps and diagrams to clarify troop movements, and turns in a 20-page report the following Friday.

Again he's called into Kissinger's office on Monday morning and again Kissinger lifts the document and drops it saying, 'So, is this the best you can do?'

And the aide suddenly realises that he hasn't done any interviews nor has he transcribed any of the primary source letters and journals. He retrieves the papers and works away on it for another week turning in a report that's nearly 100 pages long but the next Monday, it's the same dismissive question, 'So ... is this the best you can do?'

And the aide realises that he hasn't included an index, footnotes or diagrams. After two more weeks of solid work the report, in its ninth draft, is now close to 200 pages long but yet again he gets the same response from Kissinger, 'So ... is this the best you can do?'

And finally the aide loses it, 'Yes! That's it! What the hell do you want? That's the best I can do! I can't do any more! I've had it!'

Kissinger gives him a rare, slight smile, 'Good.' he says, 'Now I'll read it.'

Value clarity and simplicity above everything else. There is a tension between clarity and being concise. Obtain clarity first then, if you have time, work on reducing the amount of what you have to say.

Sir Winston Churchill is said to have spent an hour preparing for every minute of his war time radio broadcasts, refining what he wished to convey so that every sentence was as clear and concise as they could be.

Concentrate your arguments by selecting those which are most effective rather than throwing all possible points at the decision maker.

An 'everything but the kitchen sink' type approach invariably signals to the decision maker an inexperienced or unconfident advocate.

The ABC of investigation is equally a good mantra for advocates in preparing for trials, ie:

Assume nothing,

Believe nobody and

Challenge/Confirm everything.

Just as you should seek to object to your opponent's evidence you need to be prepared to rebut challenges your opponent may make as to evidence you wish to rely upon.

If you have the urge to go to the bathroom before commencing a speech should you do so?

There are two schools of thought:

One argues that you shouldn't, as it will ensure that you keep your speech short and focused.

The other fears that you will look like you are a cat on a hot tin roof and will be jumping around.

Find out which option is the best one for you!

If nerves are starting to take hold and you are feeling tense take a deep breath in and release it. Repeat this three times in succession.

At the same time, clench your hands, as tight as possible, and then let them relax too.

Never stop reading. The best way to become good at
written advocacy is to read good prose writing.

If you want to read books that may help your
advocacy look at Tips 354–365.

Your preparation should always include your having cross-referenced the topics or points you want to cover with the relevant pages from the trial bundle.

Double check you have got the right page numbers too as it doesn't help your credibility if you refer the decision maker or witness to a page that doesn't correspond to the point you are making.

A key aspect of preparing for trial is being organised. You need to organise the papers, the witnesses, the exhibits and your points.

Many advocates have a 'sick' trial. That is the trial that every time they think about it coming up it makes them feel sick.

Don't make the mistake of avoiding working on it or of putting it to the bottom of your to-do list.

Instead, be proactive and work on it regularly.

Whilst good preparation is obviously the key to being a better advocate, part of good preparation is being able to edit effectively.

Focus, in the penultimate draft of your text, on 'compression'. This is the removal of sentences and words that do not work and are unnecessary to your meaning.

Ask yourself the rhetorical question 'If I leave it out, will it create a doubt in the mind of the decision maker as to what I am saying?'

If it is possible, always seek to view the location or item involved in the trial in advance of the hearing.

What you may learn by going and looking for yourself will often be invaluable in relation to your trial preparation.

The 'backbone' of your preparation for trial will often be the creation of a timeline or chronology of events. This provides a core structure to which everything else can then be attached.

Good advocates can win many cases by having part of the other side's evidence excluded for some reason. Accordingly always include consideration of this as part of your preparation.

Advocates are often told to prepare, prepare, prepare.
What does that mean in real terms though?

Essentially it involves two key aspects:

● research, research, research; and

● rehearse, rehearse, rehearse.

An important acronym worth remembering as an advocate is CASE which stands for:

Copy

And

Steal

Everything.

The principle behind this being to watch and learn from other advocates; you don't have to constantly reinvent the wheel! A particular word, turn of phrase or analogy may be worthwhile recording and remembering for use yourself in another trial.

Courtesy involves knowing about etiquette – both
inside and outside the courtroom.

THE MECHANICS OF ADVOCACY

Write as much as possible, as the more you write, the better your writing will become.

Similarly advocacy is a skill and the more advocacy you do, and the more you reflect upon what you have done, the better your advocacy is likely to become.

Try not to sway too much when speaking. If you need to you, you can anchor yourself using, eg a lectern, but beware – this may also act, or be perceived, as a barrier between yourself and the decision maker.

To improve your oral delivery as an advocate you would do well to remember the acronym VSTEP which stands for:

Volume

Speed

Tone

Emphasis

Pauses

Change each as is necessary to make your speech interesting and engaging.

An alternative way to remember how to modulate your speech, and is an alternative to the VSTEP mnemonic, is the acronym PIP–PEP. This stands for:

Pace

Inflection

Pause

–

Pitch

Emphasis

Power

Vital for good advocacy is an understanding of the Communication Cycle.

There are four stages to the Communication Cycle that continually progress:

- First the advocate should 'Encode' the message they wish to communicate choosing the specific words and phrases.

- Then the advocate should 'Send' what they have encoded either by speaking verbally or by writing the message.

- Next the person being communicated with needs to 'Receive' what has been sent.

- Finally the recipient needs to 'Decode' that is to take meaning from what has been received.

Then the process continues once again with further 'Encoding'.

This needs to be redrawn as a flowchart, arrows going from Encode to Send to Receive to Decode.

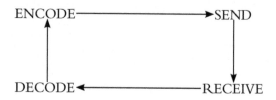

There are two predominant risks if an advocate does not understand how the Communication Cycle works:

(1)   a breakdown in communication; and/or

(2)   miscommunication.

A breakdown in communication is where something goes wrong between two of the stages in the Communication Cycle, eg when speaking on the telephone and it cuts out there will be a break between 'Sending' and 'Receiving'. Accordingly a breakdown in communication is usually fairly obvious to spot and to seek to resolve.

More insidious and dangerous is the risk of 'miscommunication' which is where the Communication Cycle appears to be working smoothly but in fact the two parties to the communication may end the conversation with different understandings of what has been conveyed.

Here is a genuine example of miscommunication in a courtroom setting:

Judge: 'Is your appearance in court today a manifestation of acquiescence on jurisdiction?'

Party to the proceedings: 'No, this is just how I dress for work.'

Encoding refers to the language, vocabulary and phrasing you use. Question construction is key so avoid using what may be classed as 'inappropriate' questions.

As an example of an inappropriate question you should avoid asking unintentionally ambiguous questions.

Recognise that everyone has their own unique 'frame of reference'; the culmination of all their experiences up to a particular moment in time. This means that whilst we may know what we are seeking to convey that is not necessarily what the recipient may interpret what we have said to have meant.

Here's an example of an ambiguous question:

> 'You've recently become friends with John, haven't you?'

Why is this ambiguous? Basically because two of the words may be interpreted in different ways by different people: 'recently' and 'friends'.

Another type of inappropriate question is the
unintentional multiple, multi-part, or compound
question, ie one where the advocate asks about more
than one fact.

For example:

'You got in your car, drove home and went
indoors, correct?'

If the witness were to simply answer 'Yes', what will
they have actually agreed to – all of the facts listed,
most of the facts or just the last fact? Only they know!

Value judgement questions are also often inappropriate.
For example:

'Is it fair to say you like your job?'

This asks for an opinion on the 'fairness' of the
assertion rather than simply asking whether the witness
likes their job.

What may be the most dangerous type of inappropriate question is the 'imperfect syllogistic' question.

Don't worry, I'll explain what this term means!

A syllogism means the adding together of two or more propositions to reach a deductive conclusion.

For example:

Proposition 1 – Socrates is a man.

Proposition 2 – All men are mortal.

Conclusion – Therefore Socrates is Mortal.

Here's an example of when an imperfect syllogistic question could be asked:

Q. You've worked at the company 20 years, correct?

A. Yes.

[Now comes the Imperfect Syllogistic Question]

Q. So, you like your job?

This is faulty logic. It has occurred because the questioner has received the fact that the witness has worked at the company for 20 years and then has applied their frame of reference concluding that if 'they', the advocate, had worked somewhere for so long it would be because they liked working in that job. They have then put this assumption/conclusion to the witness when there is every possibility that this may be a flawed conclusion and the witness does not like their job.

Imperfect Syllogistic questions occur where advocates rush. They take a fact, add their 'frame of reference', reach an assumption (often being an assumption which will assist their case) and they then put this assumption to the witness.

Imperfect syllogistic questions can usually be identified in that they start with either 'So...' or, 'I don't want to put words in your mouth but....'

Another type of potentially inappropriate question is the hypothetical question. This is where the advocate, rather than asking a question seeking to generate a fact, is instead asking a question which requires speculation or guesswork.

For example:

> 'I know you say that this didn't happen but why would Mr Cuthbert say that it did?'

This is a hypothetical question because the advocate is asking the witness to look into the mind of the other person as to their reason for not giving the same account as the witness. This is not to suggest that the issue is not a relevant one but the possible explanation needs to be obtained as a result of asking factual questions, eg 'How would you describe your relationship with Mr Cuthbert?' or 'You've never had any kind of disagreement with Mr Cuthbert, have you?'.

As far as possible seek to use active verbs in
questions, ie 'You possessed' rather than 'You were
in possession of'. It keeps the question short and will
help to focus both the witness and decision maker's
attention.

ARCC is another acronym that can help to remind you of the four elements of a persuasive voice. These are:

Articulation

Rhythm

Clarity

Colour

'Colour' refers to colour in your language, meaning, eg instead of repeatedly using 'you said' you choose more descriptive words, ie shouted, mumbled, screamed and so on.

The five most persuasive words in the English language are said to be the following:

You;

Because;

Free;

Instantly; and

New.

It might therefore be worth including one or more of these (where appropriate of course) in your submissions.

[If you are interested in why these are believed to be the most persuasive words in the English language you may wish to read the books listed in Tips 354–365 or alternatively you could just Google the topic.]

Never think that you need to show how clever you are by using complicated words and phrases. Instead always seek to use simple language.

Research by Daniel Oppenheimer titled, 'Consequences of Erudite Vernacular Utilised Irrespective of Necessity: Problems with Using Long Words Needlessly' (2006) Applied Cognitive Psychology 20: 139–156 found that simpler language led to the listener concluding that the speaker is actually more intelligent.

Try to use the philosopher Paul Grice's Four
Conversational Maxims:

(1) The maxim of Quantity – make your contribution
   as informative as is required (for the current
   purposes) without giving extraneous information.

(2) The maxim of Quality – do not say what you
   believe to be false nor say that for which you lack
   adequate evidence.

(3) The maxim of Relation – very simply, be relevant.
   Don't engage in irrelevancies.

(4) The maxim of Manner – be clear. Avoid obscurity
   of expression. Avoid ambiguity. Be brief. Be
   orderly.

Sarcasm or indignation should almost never be part of your armoury as an advocate as resorting to their use suggests an inability to be professional and to engage in the arguments on their merits.

Always strive to be professional and courteous to
your opponent. Of course you may disagree with their
argument but don't be petty or belittling and don't
make personal attacks upon them.

Do you know how many levels of listening there are? The research varies but one view is that there are four levels of listening and advocates should aim for the deepest level.

Therefore avoid the first three levels of:

Superficial or Non-listening;

Selective; and

Evaluative.

Instead aim for what may be referred to as Essential or Active listening.

Essential listening involves the listener being more focused on the speaker than they are on themselves; striving to understand the 'essence' of what the speaker is saying.

One Tip for achieving Essential listening is to be careful about rehearsing (encoding) what you want to ask whilst the witness is speaking instead of solely taking in (receiving) what the witness is saying.

Whilst interrupting the witness can sometimes be a valid cross-examination technique, be careful about interrupting a witness mid-sentence before their meaning has been made clear.

Also always be on your guard about 'hearing'
what you expect the witness to say (an example of
confirmation bias – see Tip 97) rather than what they
actually may have said.

Another error advocates regularly make is to simply listen out for points with which they can disagree. Instead make sure that you hear everything that your opponent, a witness or decision maker says.

Nervousness is a natural response to being under pressure. If you haven't been able to calm your nerves seek to transform your anxiety into excitement and use the energy this gives you.

However fast you may think you are talking you will almost always benefit by slowing down your pace.

One method for controlling your rate of speech is by speaking in phrases. This gives your listener time to first receive, then decode, what you are saying.

Accordingly your voice as an advocate is crucially important and there are a number of points to bear in mind to help you with your voice. One point to remember is to ensure that you keep your weight on both your feet should you need to stand up and address the court.

This ensures that you remain grounded and able to project your voice.

Another principle to bear in mind is to keep your
hands relaxed at your sides. When you have the
impulse to gesture let your hands help you but
be wary about holding your hands behind you as
the decision maker might wonder if you are hiding
something.

Allow yourself to take a first breath and others may
well follow. Relax your outer belly muscles and allow
each breath in. Ideally each new thought and sentence
should begin with a fresh breath.

The danger of speaking too fast is that you may leave
the decision maker behind you. Your rate of speech
will change as your thinking varies so constantly
check your pace.

Employ vocal highlighting, eg by making a sound longer, using a slightly higher pitch for a word or pausing, before or after key words. This is something we all do naturally when we are expressing something important, but sometimes we forget to do so when we're under pressure and everything may flatten out to sound the same.

Human beings use pitch as a way to inflect their thinking and make it more expressive.

Pitch can also be indicative of an emotional response. Advocates can therefore use pitch to appear more authoritative, understanding, ironic, humorous, friendly or factual.

Rhythm is also very important. Vary your rhythm as much as possible. Perhaps use monosyllables when something is really important.

Ultimately excellent advocacy may be said to be dependent upon three fundamentals:

Preparation

Personality

Presentation

Whilst CASE (see Tip 30) should always be considered never try to precisely replicate the style of any single advocate. You don't share the exact same personality as that person, nor their life's experiences.

Instead seek to create your own presentational approach from an amalgamation of those you have observed from other advocates you admire.

Ensure you make eye contact with the witness when they are answering your questions. We 'hear' more with both our eyes and ears than with our ears alone.

Make sure that your own body language isn't too
distracting to the listener. Vigorous pointing, wild arm
movements and pacing around can take away from the
message you are seeking to convey.

Still struggling to slow your speech down?

Another simple but incredibly effective solution is to count to two in your head between the end of one sentence and the next sentence you intend to say.

If you aren't familiar with the subject of linguistics, you ought to be.

Focus on the *function* of the question you intend asking as opposed to worrying too much about the *form* of that question eg:

- 'You're lying' is what is known as the declarative form;

- 'Lie to the court if you dare' is known as the imperative form; and

- 'Do you intend to continue lying to the court?' is known as the interrogative form.

However whilst there are three different *forms* all of them may have the same *function*, namely to warn the witness to think carefully about what they are saying.

Invaluable advice from Mark Twain that is worth
remembering:

> 'The right word may be effective, but no
> word was ever as effective as a rightly timed
> pause.'

Reduce the frequency of 'ums', 'ahs', 'like', 'right' and similar words from your speech as they disrupt your fluency, distract your audience and potentially undermine your credibility.

How can you do that? One method is to really *listen* to yourself talking and identify those occasions when, more often than not, you come out with one of the above 'word spacers'.

Sequencing is the term used for the arrangement of discrete pieces of information within the examination of a witness or an argument to a decision maker.

One specific model of 'sequencing' is known as the Chapter Method.

The Chapter Method organises cross examination into a cluster of favourable points (called Chapters) that ultimately help you tell the judge or jury your side of the story. It rarely will be in a simple chronological order.

To follow this method:

- Decide on a Chapter Heading which is the topic you will introduce to the witness.

- Next, at the bottom of your page, write the Chapter Conclusion – that is the point you want to be able to make about this topic in your closing speech.

- Finally, in the middle, draft a number of cross examination questions in a logical progression that lead up to, and give context to, the ultimate point you want to make.

Clint Smith, poet and teacher, has four core principles that all advocates can benefit from applying:

Read critically

Write consciously

Speak clearly

Tell your truth

One caveat to the advice to keep your hands by your sides (Tip 61) is that you can occasionally use them to help illustrate or dramatise words and thereby enhance your communication.

For example, saying 'On one hand ... but on the other hand...' whilst lifting one hand and dropping the other.

However be careful never to point directly at the decision maker with your hands as this may not be interpreted in a favourable manner!

It has been suggested that without 'presence' an advocate has nothing. However presence is a quality that can be developed over time, and comes largely as a consequence of the application of the various other qualities outlined elsewhere in this book.

Don't read out the entirety of your argument word for word nor seek to memorise the totality of what you wish to convey. Instead a common helpful approach is to remember the introduction and the last paragraph.

'Begin with the end in mind' may be a useful concept for you to focus on: ie know the last sentence you intend saying and work towards it.

Avoid unnecessary 'verbal crutches' at the start of questions, eg 'I put it to you....', 'And may I ask...' and so on, as they have no purpose save to potentially make the decision maker switch off.

Imagine how you would feel if the advocate in front of you used the expression, 'And it would be right to say...' eighteen times during the course of one submission.

Avoid jargon if at all possible and be careful in your use of acronyms and abbreviations since the decision maker(s) may not be familiar with them.

Whatever you have to say – strive to make it
interesting! If a decision maker is bored by what you
are saying they are likely to switch off.

Develop your understanding and command of grammar. Don't say 'can' when what you ought to be saying is 'may'. However don't stray too far and become a pedant worrying about splitting your infinitives (a concept more appropriate for Latin than applicable to modern languages).

Try always to be explicit. Never assume that the judge will work out what it is you are saying or what you are asking for.

Restrain your own emotions as an advocate. Seek instead to adopt a posture of respectful intellectual equality with the judge.

PSYCHOLOGY

Accept that you're human and that everyone makes mistakes. Don't bother apologising for stumbles in any submissions or arguments you make – just move on.

Never be afraid of silence. If you are dealing with a witness from whom you are seeking to get more information and they are being reticent, pausing after their answer and waiting expectantly before you ask your next question can lead the witness to add a further comment that they might not otherwise have made.

Such pauses can also act to underline the last answer given by a witness as well as giving the decision maker time to reflect upon it.

Various research studies have confirmed that getting someone to say 'Yes' to a series of statements makes that person more likely to agree with later propositions that are put to them.

If a witness you have called on behalf of your client begins to get anxious don't respond in a like manner and get anxious yourself.

Instead remember that 'calm creates calm' and by emanating calm yourself they may begin to relax more themselves.

When making oral submissions save your time and persuade by rhyme. Research studies show that people are more likely to view assertions which rhyme as more accurate than those which don't.

For example you will likely recall the famous assertion used by Johnnie Cochrane in the trial of OJ Simpson, 'If it doesn't fit, you must acquit'. (This is what he actually said as opposed to the oft-misquoted, 'If the gloves don't fit, you must acquit'.)

Aim to establish rapport with a witness as this will
generate more information from the witness and may
make them be less antagonistic towards you.

There are a number of steps an advocate may take to develop rapport with a witness. The first step is always to plan beforehand and to ask yourself what do you already know about the witness?

Further steps to consider are:

- Mirroring the witness's posture, gestures, facial expressions, rate of speech and breathing (not mimicking precisely as this may be a recipe for disaster!).

- Nodding your head as the witness speaks can also assist in demonstrating that you are listening and can act as encouragement to what they are saying.

Personality mirroring is also worth trying which is when the advocate seeks to match the thought processes and style of communication the witness prefers by perhaps mirroring the tonality of their voice.

Another aspect to building rapport is to empathise with the witness.

For example ask yourself,

- What is the main aim of most witnesses?

- What preconceptions do they bring into court?

A few final generic points for rapport building:

● Be polite, even-tempered, objective and confident.

● Avoid crossing your arms or not looking at the witness. Doing this can send out signals of disinterest and even dislike of the witness which may prompt them to respond negatively.

Advocates should avoid 'Confirmation Bias'. This is a tendency to favour information that confirms their own hypotheses and beliefs.

However advocates should seek to exploit the situation when witnesses have themselves relied upon their own confirmation bias.

The British politician Lord Molson gave a wonderful description of confirmation bias when he said:

> 'I will look at any additional evidence to confirm the opinion to which I have already come.'

When dealing with witnesses who are potential liars,
advocates need to recognise that there are five ways
someone may seek to lie or deceive:

1   Denial;

2   Exaggeration/Minimisation;

3   Omission;

4   Euphemisms; and

5   Fabrication.

Denials are a simple refutation of the truthful statement. For example in response to the question:

'You went to the bar?'

The witness might respond with the simple denial:

'I didn't go to the bar.'

When the witness had in reality been in the bar drinking all night.

Exaggeration/Minimisation involves the witness seeking to distract from the truth by either embellishing or downplaying what they did.

For example taking the same scenario the witness might instead say:

> 'Yes I went to the bar but I only had a couple of drinks'.

Omission is the deliberate absence of a statement. It is leaving out the crucial information.

Again using the same example the witness might say:

> 'Well it had been my intention to go to the bar'.

In this instance the witness has essentially failed to answer the question.

Euphemism or 'special language' is where the witness exploits ambiguous language to their own ends.

Using the same example the witness might say:

'I did not go to a drinking establishment'

Here the witness has deliberately avoided using the word 'bar'.

Lastly comes Fabrication, what most people instinctively think of as a 'lie'. This is the creation of a separate reality, a fiction.

Again using the same example the witness might reply:

'No, I was working in the office all night'.

It is incredibly easy for any witness to tell a lie because we are experts at doing so. We learn to tell lies as soon as we learn to communicate. Don't believe me? Well let me tell you about Koko.

Koko, a gorilla, was well known for having a 1,000-word sign language vocabulary. After she learned how to communicate with her caretakers at the Gorilla Foundation in Northern California she requested a kitten as a pet.

One day whilst alone Koko managed to rip a sink out of the wall in her habitat. When her human caretakers returned and asked Koko who had ripped out the sink Koko signed, 'The cat did it.'

Whilst, therefore, it is easy to *tell* a lie, what is much harder for anyone to do is to *maintain* the lie. Therefore if you believe a witness may be lying to you ask them more questions, probe their account more fully. This will increase what is known as their cognitive load and errors may start to creep into their account.

Here are some possible indicators of deceit to listen out for:

- The witness avoids getting to the main issue of the question;

- The witness deflects responding by querying the question asked or by simply not answering the question;

- The witness repeats the question asked (although the advocate should always first consider whether or not their question was indeed unclear or unintentionally ambiguous)';

- The witness uses 'distancing language' eg 'we/its' instead of 'I/my';

- The witness uses passive instead of active language eg – 'the transaction was authorised' rather than 'I authorised the transaction'.

An important maxim to bear in mind is that a witness whose evidence suffers from no internal inconsistency (ie that everything they have said is consistent with everything else) is more likely to be judged by the decision maker to be correct and truthful than a witness whose evidence appears to contradict itself.

Similarly the witness whose evidence is consistent
with the documents in the case is more likely to be
considered to be correct and credible by the decision
maker.

Whilst things may look bad for you sometimes just one unassailable piece of evidence may be able to be used to reveal to the decision maker what the true facts are; eg, despite overwhelming evidence suggesting X committed an offence, a DNA analysis of a sample recovered from the scene demonstrates that Y must have been the perpetrator.

Always start strong!

Psychologists have confirmed that first impressions are important so the first 30 seconds of each submission and examination are critical.

If you are a new and anxious advocate develop an 'alter ego' for court to overcome stage fright, ie 'fake it until you make it'.

Speak with passion. When people sense you really care and believe in something, and want to convey that passion to them, they'll pay attention.

Don't be afraid of *occasionally* repeating yourself.
Repetition, both visual and verbal, can help jurors to
retain and recall key information (but be alive to Tip
327).

When people hear new, unfamiliar terms they become so distracted that they are unlikely to pay attention to (ie receive) the next seven words.

Within ethical constraints it may be legitimate to seek to elicit anger from a witness since angry people often don't think before speaking.

In Western societies always look your decision maker in the eye when talking to them. Whilst it is an urban myth that liars won't look you in the eye when talking to you the myth still perpetuates.

Frankness is an invaluable quality as an advocate.
Never be afraid to tell those that have instructed you
information they may not want to hear.

Another important psychological concept advocates should be familiar with is 'cognitive dissonance'. This is where an individual cannot accept an occurrence or assertion because to do so would be to challenge their way of looking at the world.

For example, the immediate response of most managers to an allegation of wrongdoing by a member of their staff, whom they like and have worked with for many years, is to dispute the validity of the allegation. This is because to accept it as potentially accurate would mean that the manager's world view is wrong, that they are a poor judge of character. They cannot accept this and therefore could be described as suffering with cognitive dissonance.

All advocates ought to be familiar with the work of the
psychologist Elizabeth Loftus, especially her research
in relation to the reconstructive nature of memory and
the way in which question construction can impact
upon the subsequent recollection of a witness.

Be willing to smile at the decision maker. Research studies suggest that smiling is the highest positive emotional gesture we can make.

When you make mistakes, as we all do, don't beat yourself up over them. Reflect on them and learn from them.

As Piet Hein put it:

> 'The road to wisdom? Well, it's plain and simple to express:
> Err, and err, and err again. But less, and less, and less.'

QUESTIONING: EXAMINATION-IN-CHIEF/DIRECT EXAMINATION

When questioning witnesses always remember to KISS:

Keep

It

Short and

Simple.

Make use of wide open questions.

One way to remember wide open questions is by use of the acronym TED which stands for: **T**ell, **E**xplain and **D**escribe.

[On a separate note all good advocates should be familiar with the website www.ted.com. Not only will you see examples of excellent advocacy, presentations and rhetoric but you will also learn information about other subjects that will assist you as an advocate!]

A second set of questions used in direct examination/ examination–in–chief can be classed as open.

A further simply way to remember open questions is by the acronym 5WH which stands for:

Who,

What,

Where,

When,

Why,

How.

(Or if you prefer you may want to memorise the following extract from Rudyard Kipling's poem *"I keep six honest...."*)

> 'I keep six honest serving-men
>
> (They taught me all I knew);
>
> Their names are What and Why and When
>
> And How and Where and Who.'

Also appropriate for direct examination/examination-in-chief are what may be described as 'closed' questions.

The purpose of closed questions is to clarify or confirm a fact that the witness has already given.

For example:

'Was anyone else present?'

'Did you say anything else?'

A difficult habit to avoid is the 'OK' syndrome.

If you're in need of self-assurance you'll say 'OK' as a response to almost every answer you receive from a witness.

This sounds and appears needy and may not help to build your credibility with the decision maker.

Ban yourself from asking the unfocused and complacent:

'And what happened next?'

when conducting either direct/examination-in-chief or cross-examination, as to do so risks losing control of the witness's evidence.

'Reflective questioning' is a technique whereby the pace of the conversation is used to evoke the time matters took or the intensity of events. If you speak faster it may feel to those listening as though events are closer together and more intense.

Ensure you get the details when you are asking questions in direct examination/examination-in-chief.

For example, let's assume that you have asked, 'What did the man do?' and you get the response, 'He hit me in the face'.

What details doesn't the decision maker know?

- They don't know what the man hit the witness with – ie his hand, a weapon or something else.

- They don't know how many times the witness was hit.

- They don't know how the witness felt about it.

And so on.

Make the account come alive to the listener.

The way to elicit specific details is by means of a series of incremental questions that build the picture you are trying to paint piece by piece like a builder would build a house, brick by brick.

Re-examination should not be done unless necessary. There are two scenarios when it may be necessary:

- when a point has become confused in cross-examination that needs to be clarified; and

- to seek to re-establish the credibility of the witness in some way if they have been discredited during the cross-examination.

QUESTIONING: CROSS-EXAMINATION

In cross-examination the vast majority of advocacy trainers will advise you to focus on *telling* the witness the answer you want rather than asking them a question, eg:

'You were at home, correct?' not,

'Were you at home?'

This is to ensure that you maintain control of the witness. Whilst telling does not apply to questioning in direct examination/examination-in-chief, maintaining control of the witness does.

[A caveat here is that this technique should not be used with witnesses who are in any way vulnerable due to their age, learning difficulties or similar, because for them such a technique is powerfully suggestive and linguistically complex. As a result improper use of this technique could lead to a warped account being obtained from a vulnerable witness. See amongst others Tips 150–153, 155 and 359.]

Avoid the common mistake of asking double negative questions eg:

'You didn't not go to the park, did you?'

There will always be an easier way to ask the question, for example:

'You went to the park, correct?'

When cross-examining, if part of your aim is to seek to undermine a witness's credibility, there are three main lines of attack.

Either you will wish to suggest that the witness is:

(a) being dishonest,

(b) inaccurate/inconsistent; or

(c) biased.

Or you may seek to suggest some combination of (a), (b) and (c).

Don't emphasise the *cross* in cross-examination.
Cross-examination is best undertaken politely and
courteously. Don't immediately go for the witness's
jugular!

In cross-examination advocates ought to use predominantly closed, leading questions (also known as 'tag' questions) as the way to control the witness.

There are four main ways to structure such questions.

The first way to structure closed leading questions is:

Positive Assertion, Positive Tag, eg:

> 'You got in the car, correct?'

The second method for structuring closed, leading questions in cross-examination is:

Positive Assertion and Negative Tag, eg:

> 'You got in the car, didn't you?'

The third method of structuring closed, leading questions is simply to put a Positive Assertion in a questioning tone:

> 'You got in the car?'

NB Some judges may assert that you are not asking a question but making a statement in this third method. If so, stick to using 'tag' questions.

The fourth method of structuring closed, leading questions in XX is:

Negative Assertion, Positive Tag, eg:

> 'You didn't get in the car, did you?'

In cross-examination never ask a question where you
care what the answer is going to be. Whatever answer
you receive you should be able to deal with it.

This is a development from the more commonly known
assertion:

> 'Don't ask a question to which you don't know
> the answer.'

Advocates regularly ask questions to which they don't
know the answer – the secret is not to be concerned
whether the answer is yes or no (which the answer will
be as you'll be asking closed leading questions, won't
you) but to have a plan of attack regardless of the
witness's response.

In cross-examination an advocate may seek to either:

(1) confront the witness with evidence that is inconsistent with their account;

(2) insinuate another version of events; or

(3) probe the witness's evidence for flaws.

Cross-examination should never be an opportunity for the witness to give their evidence again. Don't bother asking them for facts the court already knows.

Never forget, once you lose control of a witness, it will be hard to get it back.

One way to handle someone you consider to be an 'evasive' witness is to simply re-ask the question you had previously asked verbatim. Of course to do so means that you must be able to remember the precise question that you ask at any time.

Another method for handling an evasive witness is to re-ask the question you had asked but in a way that demonstrates that the witness is seeking to evade answering it.

Alternatively you can simply point out to an evasive witness that you are going to re-ask the question as they haven't answered it (although be careful here as you may be accused by the decision maker of having 'commented').

Cross-examining expert witnesses presents its own demands. There are five ways to undertake this:

(1) Challenge any opinions they give which fall outside their own specific area of expertise.

(2) Challenge their actual expertise, ie do they have the experience or knowledge required to give the particular opinion they have provided?

(3) Challenge their preparation or the procedures that were involved in reaching their conclusions – perhaps they made mistakes?

(4) Challenge any assumptions that they have made in order to reach their conclusion – did they consider alternative assumptions and, if so, were they wrong to dismiss them?

(5) Invite them to speculate. Ask, if certain facts were different, would their conclusions alter?

Never, ever, argue with a witness. The witness may disagree with what you say (in fact they almost certainly will in cross-examination) but do not enter into a debate, discussion or argument with them. If you do argue with them you run the risk of losing your credibility with the decision maker as a result.

One cross-examination tactic is known as 'Rapid fire' questioning.

In this technique as soon as the witness has answered a question the advocate immediately asks another question without pausing.

This gives the witness little time to recover after encoding and sending their response such that they may then rush the receiving and decoding of the next question and not necessarily answer as best as they might.

Of course a disadvantage of this technique is that the advocate similarly has little time to decode the response from the witness and to encode his or her questions hence the reason why the advocate generally should focus on obtaining only 'Yes' or 'No' answers.

When cross-examining a witness one particular aspect you may wish to undertake is the impeachment of a witness where you demonstrate that they have changed their account.

This is where a witness has given a different account in court from an account they have previously given and you wish to rely upon the earlier account.

There are two ways to remember how to undertake impeachment: CAPRI and the 3Cs.

CAPRI is an acronym for: Confirm, Accept, Produce, Ring fence and Inconsistency.

CONFIRM involves getting the witness to repeat the statement he or she has just made during evidence in the trial.

ACCEPT involves asking the witness to agree that they made a prior statement (although not yet asking about the substance of that prior statement).

Next you should **P**RODUCE, that is show the witness, their prior statement.

RING FENCE involves confirming with the witness that they signed to say that the contents of the prior statement you've shown them were true.

INCONSISTENCY (or **I**MPEACHMENT) means that once the witness admits making the prior statement you, or the witness, read aloud the inconsistency in the statement to the jury.

Another way to remember how to impeach is the 3 Cs: Commit, Credit and Confront.

Commit is getting the witness to confirm what they have just said.

Credit involves having the witness accept they made the earlier statement by, if necessary, showing them what they said.

Confront is then demonstrating that the two statements are contradictory.

If you suspect a witness is lying (especially if they may be using euphemism or exaggeration/minimisation) you can intensify your questioning by using terms such as 'specifically' eg 'You specifically said 'X', didn't you?'

Now for tips on handling vulnerable witnesses, ie those who through age or some form of learning difficulty, mental health problems or trauma are at a disadvantage to others when giving their evidence.

The first and most important is to avoid what are known as 'tag' questions, ie those questions set out at Tip 135!

The reason why this form of question should not be used when dealing with vulnerable witnesses is because they are powerfully suggestive (hence why they have traditionally been used in trials) but also because they are linguistically complex. There is therefore a real risk that vulnerable witnesses will not give a truthful answer but will be intimidated or confused by the response required.

Another key consideration when dealing with vulnerable witnesses is to speak slowly. Avoid using the 'rapid fire' technique as vulnerable witnesses need time to process what has been said to them.

A simple general rule is to give a vulnerable witness six or more seconds to consider and respond to what has been said to them.

More frequent breaks than might be the norm will also undoubtedly be helpful to vulnerable witnesses.

You may wish to consider using diagrams or other visual aids as part of your questioning especially with vulnerable witnesses but all witnesses are likely to benefit from this approach (see Tip 185 also).

Another point which is of general application is
to sign-post topics and not to jump around the
chronology of events, eg 'I now want to move to ask
you about the meeting on the 1st of May 2014'.

As much as possible avoid abstract concepts and euphemisms with vulnerable witnesses. Keep the focus on concrete subjects but if you do need to use abstract concepts clarify them by giving real-life examples.

Don't repeat questions to vulnerable witnesses.

Why not? Simply because a vulnerable witness is liable to believe that you didn't like the first answer they gave so they had best give you a different answer of which you will approve.

If you are unlikely to elicit evidence on
cross-examination to help your case, or to hinder your
opponent's, don't ask for that witness to attend court
and give them the chance to repeat damaging testimony
in person (perhaps to even more devastating effect!)

If a witness called by your opponent testified unfavourably to your opponent's case during their examination-in-chief/direct examination don't go over the same testimony again on cross-examination.

If you do you may give them the opportunity to then explain what they said and put right any damage that may have been caused by their initial statement.

Whilst putting colour into what you say is generally a good idea especially for speeches, during cross-examination be careful not to use adjectives or adverbs needlessly, as doing so can give the witness an opportunity to say more than just 'yes' or 'no'.

For example, if you suggested:

'You then shouted to her to stop, didn't you?'

instead of:

'You then told her to stop, didn't you?'

There is a risk that the witness's response may be:

'I never shouted at her'.

Always be ready to abandon a line of questioning if you:

(a) get a surprisingly favourable response; or

(b) get progressively worse answers.

Mis-stating facts to a witness is a bad tactic to employ. It may make the witness argue with you and is likely to be resented by the decision maker.

If you want to force a witness to concede a point you'll need to close off all possible 'escape routes' before seeking to press home the point.

Do not cross-examine simply to please your client.
You are the expert as to the law and trial strategy – not
them.

Would you expect your client to tell a surgeon how to
go about operating on them?

Another quote from Howard L Nations employing the
use of the Rule of 3 (see Tip 305):

> 'The three most important aspects of
> conducting cross-examination are control,
> control, and control'.

Avoid asking any unnecessary questions during cross-examination as you will only be deemed as good as your last series of questions.

If you give a witness a choice between blaming
themselves or blaming someone else for an error that
has occurred they will nearly always blame someone
else. Why? Cognitive dissonance again! (see Tip 117).

Never confuse quantity with quality in cross-examination. Just because you are asking lots of questions does not mean that your cross-examination is being effective.

Witnesses don't have to use exactly the same words every time they speak. You may look foolish if you seek to impeach a minor difference in what they have said on two separate occasions.

Remember that you should only impeach specific factual assertions, not inferences that you may have made from the witness's evidence. This is because you may have drawn an incorrect inference.

Do your utmost to avoid 'criss-crossing' between themes or issues about which you are cross-examining. If you don't you run the risk of confusing the witness and/or the decision maker.

Try to avoid making a witness upset to the point of
tears as this may well invite sympathy for them from
the decision maker.

As a general rule ensure that you have had the witness commit to certain facts you need before you proceed into asking them about riskier subjects where they are more likely to disagree with you.

One particular type of witness you may encounter is someone who is narcissistic (ie they have an overly inflated view of their abilities, personality or character). There are a variety of ways to deal with this witness but fundamentally they can be summed up either as exposing them as being flawed in some way or by belittling them.

There is said to be a 'classic format' for structuring the cross-examination of a witness:

Start friendly.

Get points that build your case rather than attack your opponent's.

Bring out anything which is incontrovertible which helps you or hurts your opponent.

Challenge the witness's recollection.

Impeach them where possible and appropriate.

End on a high.

Never forget – more cross-examinations are suicidal than they are homicidal! Always ask yourself whether or not you really do need to cross-examine a particular witness.

Cross-examination has been described by some people as 'the firing of bullets with the intention to inflict damage'. Realise that sometimes you will miss the target!

Whilst first impressions are important so too are final impressions. Don't finish a cross-examination after receiving an adverse answer.

If you get an answer that may be helpful to you in cross-examination leave it alone. Resist the inevitable temptation to follow it up with another question because the witness may well realise that they have made a mistake and somehow seek to qualify the previous answer that they gave to you.

Another cross-examination technique that may sometimes be effective is called the 'Scatter Gun' approach. This is where the advocate jumps from one topic to another without a clear pattern. Whilst this goes against the Chapter Method (and Tip 170) it may be effective with some witnesses who seek to pre-empt the conclusions you are trying to reach.

DECISION MAKERS

Decision makers, when considering a witness's
evidence, will always believe that the usual is more
likely to be what occurred than the unusual. Therefore
always strive to suggest that your account of events is
the more common, usual occurrence.

Always remember it is 'horses for courses'.

Tailor your submissions to the judge as each decision maker has their own approach, knowledge and frame of reference.

As an unknown commentator once said:

> 'Good lawyers know the law; great lawyers know the judge'.

A particularly important type of inference to focus the
decision maker on is the 'goal' inference. This is where
having identified a witness's goal or aim you are able
to suggest that they took action in furtherance of that
goal, eg lied to the court.

If the judge asks you a question always answer it directly. If necessary start with a yes or no then add any qualification that is required.

Do not belittle circumstantial evidence.

This is the indirect evidence of a proposition or event which merely requires greater corroboration than direct evidence of the occurrence.

Decision makers, like all human beings, enjoy solving puzzles so they will enjoy putting the pieces together themselves if you let them.

Don't force a witness to describe something that they may be able to point out from a photograph or refer to on a map or plan.

Human beings are generally a visual species so engage with that aspect of the decision maker.

If you make a mistake as an advocate admit it – don't try to cover it up with a poor explanation or excuse.

Stop speaking immediately when a judge asks a
question. Never speak over them. Once you have
answered their question find a way to get back to the
point you were making before their question.

Never display frustration with a judge when making a submission to them. That means not engaging in sighing, rolling your eyes, or shaking your head.

Often, when people say to a judge 'with respect'
or 'respectfully' it's in fact when they're not being
respectful. Consider whether it's ever wise to use such
an expression.

Be careful that the decision maker doesn't form the view that you are trying to 'trick' a witness, as, should they reach such a conclusion, they may start to doubt your credibility as an advocate.

Generally avoid intentionally using humour in a
courtroom as it can often undermine any rapport you
may have created with the decision maker.

Never whine. Nothing will make the court stop listening to you more quickly than should you engage in whining.

Understanding your audience is clearly crucial to
any advocate and essentially there are three ways to
achieve this:

THINK, RESEARCH and ASK.

Always consider what level of knowledge the judge/
decision maker starts the case with?

Determine whether the decision maker is likely to be appreciative of what you have to say or whether they are likely to be hostile towards it?

Think about what expectations the decision maker is likely to have at the start of your submissions?

Another consideration is what might the decision
maker find irritating or unconvincing in what you have
to say? Then consider how you can deal with that
view.

Always consider what the decision maker's biggest
concerns are likely to be and what unanswered
questions about the issues they could have such that
you may do your best to answer them.

Always remember that 'I don't know' is a much better response to a question a judge may ask you than simply making something up.

If your opponent objects to a question you ask, and the judge agrees with them, aim to rephrase the question – don't argue with the judge.

If you're interrupted by a question from the judge aim to answer it immediately (see Tip 183). However if that is impossible say that you'll deal with it later and make a note to ensure that you do!

If something is your fault, whether deliberate or
unintentional, apologise immediately. It can be
irritating if an advocate prevaricates.

Juries try to fit each bit of evidence into a cohesive story. If they can't do that, evidence which doesn't fit will either tend to get dismissed or the story will be reframed to incorporate the evidence.

Juries tend to discount expert testimony unless it is
firmly rooted in the factual evidence.

Never underestimate the importance of watching the judge in a jury trial. His or her reaction is often being closely observed by the jury so keep your eyes up and look around.

Never forget that you are in court to reason with the decision maker – accordingly you should not show yourself to be an unreasonable individual.

Seek to influence each element of the 'OODA Loop' that all decision makers engage in.

OODA stands for:

Observe,

Orientate,

Decide before taking

Action.

Utilise 'trivial persuasion' by eliciting a minor but highly specific detail from a witness as this will raise their perceived credibility in the eyes of the decision maker.

Keep in mind that the witness is likely to be viewed as the 'underdog' by the jury in your interaction with them and their sympathies will ordinarily be with the witness at the start of your questioning.

Never interrupt a judge as he or she is asking a question, even if you think you know what they are going to ask you. Always wait for the entire question.

Think about the volume of your voice. Be sure
you can be heard. However, don't start yelling at
judges. Unsurprisingly this can be considered to be
aggressive and unpersuasive.

Everyone is more likely to be persuaded by someone we like or admire as opposed to someone we dislike. Therefore whilst some advocates may make a career at baiting judges you'll often get more success with the carrot than the stick.

If possible evoke indignation from the decision maker
on your behalf rather than displaying it yourself.

Inaccuracies usually result from either a deliberate mis-statement or carelessness. Whatever the cause, your inaccuracies will damage your credibility as an advocate with the decision maker.

Never underestimate the intelligence of jurors.

If you feel nervous or anxious when speaking always remember that your listener doesn't want you to fail, they want to understand what you are saying.

Never assume that, simply because there has been
no evidence presented about a fact, the decision
maker isn't thinking about it. Where there are gaps in
knowledge it is normal human nature for a decision
maker to seek to fill them.

Duration can be an important unconscious determining factor for decision makers. If you spend longer on a particular topic, this may implicitly indicate to them that this is a crucial area they should focus on.

Try to work out the questions the decision maker may
be asking themselves so that you can ensure that
your submissions answer those questions. Don't try to
avoid dealing with them!

If the decision maker answers the question you have framed for them they ought to reach the conclusion you urge them to.

Although you should speak with passion (see Tip 111) do not speak in such a way that the decision maker starts to doubt your professional independence. If they question your professional independence your credibility will be damaged and it will be much harder to ultimately persuade them of the veracity of your argument in that case.

Always be polite and courteous to court staff. They may not be the decision maker but their opinion of you could easily be conveyed to the decision maker which could itself have an impact on how the decision maker views you, your credibility and your argument.

Try to ensure that any argument you make will harmonise with the decision maker's own frame of reference or script. The more it doesn't harmonise the greater the risk of cognitive dissonance (see Tip 117) and the more you will struggle to convince them of your argument.

Generally judges are motivated by fairness to the litigants before them, a socially desirable outcome to the case and, where it applies, the laying down of a rule which will provide fairness in the future. Bear this in mind when making your submissions.

Never praise a judge's question. Of course it is
relevant and appropriate – why else would he or she
have asked it?

TRIAL STRATEGY

Identify your opponent's greatest asset and seek to use it against them. Convert their strength into a weakness.

Your reputation is key (see Tip 221). As US judge
Breitel has said:

'Arguing with a bad reputation is like climbing
a glass mountain in shoes covered with oil'.

Never, therefore, choose to put one short term advantage above your long term reputation.

One witness to a fact is adequate; two witnesses and a corroborating document are persuasive. Your goal is to make your case persuasive, never merely adequate.

For both greater impact and an increased likelihood
of the decision maker retaining their evidence, seek to
start with your most important witness and end your
case with your second most important witness (unless
doing so may undermine the logical progression of the
case).

Be careful about using exaggeration or hyperbole in your speeches. If you say outrageous things that aren't true the decision maker will doubt your credibility.

Never forget that, as the advocate, you are not the focus of the case. It isn't what you think or believe that matters, it is what the decision maker concludes.

A good advocate knows when their case is unlikely to win. Then they put all of their efforts into persuading their opponent to settle on the best possible terms.

Be careful about responding too quickly when
your opponent or the judge invites you to make a
concession. Once made it will be impossible to recover
lost ground.

Two simple but crucial rules:

(1) never underestimate your opponent; and

(2) never be late for court (the earlier you arrive the better!).

Enhance the credibility of a witness's account,
where possible, by getting them to explain why they
remember what they have described and how they can
be sure of what they have told the court.

As much as possible seek to agree admissions and
undisputed facts with your opponent as this will assist
you in focusing your argument, in limiting your
cross-examination, and will help the decision maker in
determining the case.

How to decide whether details you are seeking from a
witness are relevant or not? Ask yourself whether that
detail will contribute to the persuasiveness of your case
theory. If it will then draw the detail out, if it won't
then don't ask for it.

Have clear transitions between topics. It will be easier
for both the witness and the decision maker to follow
the account being given if they understand when one
episode or segment has ended and when another has
begun.

If you think that the members of the jury may have
difficulty understanding a legal concept make an
analogy to some common experience which they ought
to be more familiar with.

Remember Sun Tzu's assertion:

'Tactics without strategy is the noise before defeat'.

Just because you may not be addressing the decision maker doesn't mean that you are not 'on stage' and working. Remember you are always being watched and evaluated by others in court.

Always aim to arrive at court not just early but with everything you need. Don't leave matters to the last minute. After all, if you fail to prepare, prepare to fail!

You must be absolutely clear as to the theory of your case and keep it uppermost in your mind throughout the trial.

Be flexible – don't be an advocate who is unable to adapt.

Resist the temptation to offer several alternative
theories and avoid becoming bogged down in
reviewing uncontested or trivial matters (see Tip 15).

During a trial, make it a habit to get to court not just early but always before your opponent, every day. This may have the beneficial effect of making your adversary perceive you as perpetually ready!

Should the opposing advocate falter or blunder during a hearing don't gloat – you could be next! However, if they are 'digging a hole' for themselves, let them carry on – you're not there to save them.

As a general rule, when you run into a non-responsive witness, get control of them yourself. Don't ask the court to control the witness for you ie don't ask the judge to make the witness answer the question. Doing so may make you appear weak or unable to control the witness.

When you want the jury to see something make sure that all the jurors can see it.

In trials help your client to maintain control of their
emotions – without resorting to the use of alcohol or
some other form of medication!

Clarify a witness's non-verbal conduct and gestures
in case the decision maker hasn't spotted it, perhaps
because their attention is temporarily focused
elsewhere, eg:

> 'You have raised your right hand with a closed
> fist, is that correct?'

Don't pass notes, whisper or tug the sleeve of
co-counsel or lead counsel when they are examining
a witness. It distracts both the examiner and any
jurors and gives the appearance that you may lack
confidence in the person carrying out the examination.

If you are trying to suggest that the witness is a liar, you'll be more successful if you establish that the witness has a motive for lying.

Don't change your personality during a trial unless it is a genuine response to surprising testimony. False reactions are obvious to a jury and again will hurt your credibility with them.

Try not to be aloof during a trial. Get to know the courtroom personnel as best you are able to as, during a trial, you can never have too many friends!

The purpose of most types of litigation is not to satisfy the advocate's personal curiosity about what might have 'really happened'. Accordingly don't get fixated on issues that are not relevant to the key disputed points in the case.

Try to recruit independent witnesses to your cause as they are more likely to be believed than one who is perceived as having a motive to lie or to give a biased account.

Don't fight hypotheticals the judge may ask you, nor should you try to avoid responding to them. Give an answer to the hypothetical question and if that potentially undermines your position distinguish the hypothetical situation from your case.

Be wary about suggesting your opponent's case lacks any merit whatsoever; if the court disagrees with you it may damage your credibility.

Don't let your opponent re-characterise your position as being more extreme than you had set it out. Set the record straight if necessary.

Never let the vehemence of your opponent's attacks
drive you to less defensible ground. Don't feel that
you must immediately give way to their arguments as
if you do you may find yourself having ended up in a
situation whereby your argument is all but lost.

Try never to accuse an opponent of outright sharp practice. Always work on the assumption that they have made a genuine error rather than that they have been deliberately underhand or dishonest.

Do not over-act. The courtroom is often described as being akin to being on stage but don't ham it up!

It doesn't matter which side your client is on, what matters is who controls the battleground. As the eminent advocate Clarence Darrow put it:

'I'll gladly take either side of a case as long as I may pick the issues.'

Remember that you're not trying to talk witnesses into
changing their testimony or confessing to wrongdoing
(you aren't Perry Mason, Rumpole of the Bailey
or Alan Shore). Instead you simply wish to show to
the decision maker that the witness is unreliable and
therefore that their evidence lacks credibility.

Look out for facts which a witness gives that either
are incapable of being proved or are, on the face of
it, highly implausible. Both are useful areas to exploit
during cross-examination.

The source of information is often forgotten over
time with the listener remembering what was said
as opposed to who said it. If therefore you want to
undermine particular evidence due to the unreliability
of a particular witness you must ensure that you remind
the decision maker of which witness gave that piece of
evidence.

CONSTRUCTING ARGUMENTS, RHETORIC AND SUBMISSIONS

Insecurity means that some advocates begin their submissions with excuses eg 'I haven't had much time to prepare'. This won't make the judge be gentle with you but could instead raise the expectation in them that you are going to do a poor job.

'Apposition' is an important rhetorical device whereby the placing of important facts in a certain order emphasises the relationship of those facts.

For example:

'The defendant, a man of unblemished good character,...'

emphasises that when thinking about the defendant the decision maker ought to keep in mind that he has never previously been convicted of any crime and therefore is unlikely to be guilty on this occasion.

Never assert to the court, 'My client will say...', as they invariably won't!

Avoid three common errors when you make
submissions namely:

    using cliches,

    being sarcastic; and, perhaps worst of all,

    rambling.

In cases where a person's identification is in issue remember the acronym ADVOKATE:

A refers to the Amount of time the witness had to see the person relevant to events. The less time the less accurate a witness may be.

D stands for the Distance between the witness and the person they first saw. The further the distance the harder it is to be accurate.

V is for Visibility, that is the conditions that existed at the time of the original sighting, eg was it sunny or raining, night or day. If the observation occurred at night, when it was dark and raining, it may be harder for the witness to have got a good look at the person.

O refers to the witness's Observation and whether it was impeded by other people or objects or whether it was clear. Again if there were barriers between the witness and the person they saw then again they may not have got a good look at the individual.

K is for Knowledge of the identified person and whether the witness had prior knowledge which might have impacted on the identification. If the person they saw was a stranger, as opposed to someone whom they had previously had contact with, they may not have picked up on the person's characteristics.

A is for Any special reason to remember the person seen eg a tattoo, scar or similar distinguishing mark. Again if the person is lacking in any specific distinguishing features the risk of a misidentification increases.

T stands for the Time which has elapsed between a witness's original sighting of the relevant person and their subsequent identification of whom they assert was the person they originally saw. The longer the period of time that has elapsed the greater the potential that someone's memory will have degraded and the greater the risk of error.

And finally the **E** stands for any Error, ie discrepancy between the original description given by the witness and the appearance of the person they subsequently identified as being the same person they saw on the first occasion.

Using fewer words in your submissions can actually build trust in the decision maker. In contrast if you include words that don't convey meaning (ie if you waffle or ramble) you can reduce the reader's/ listener's interest.

For every argument that opposes your position give three positive arguments in favour of your case. A 3:1 ratio is much more likely to persuade the decision maker of your case.

Advocates ought to be aware of, and use, the
rhetorical triangle, ie all arguments should include
logos (logic), pathos (emotion) and ethos (credibility).

An example of an argument that includes all three
elements of logos, pathos and ethos would be as
follows:

> 'As your lawyer (ethos), I have to tell you
> that if you don't give evidence, you're going
> to lose your case (pathos) as the decision
> maker won't have the chance to weigh up your
> account (logos).'

Logos involves logical appeals to our reasoning. This means making arguments which are 'sound' (see Tip 290) and 'valid' (see Tip 289) avoiding fallacious arguments.

A fallacy or fallacious argument essentially is one which involves an error in reasoning and is separate and distinct from a factual error.

Ethos relies on your own credibility and involves appeals to the decision maker's good will, their practical wisdom and their ideas of virtue.

Pathos appeals to a decision maker's emotional nature.
As Blaise Pascal said:

> 'The heart has reasons that the mind knows not
> of'.

There are five principles to rhetoric in practice.

The first is **Invention** this involves brainstorming the subject including considering what your opponent's argument is likely to be.

The second rhetorical principle is **Arrangement** of your argument. This can be further sub-divided into the following elements:

- introduction;

- statement of the facts;

- division of your ideas/arguments;

- proof that supports your ideas;

- refutation of your opponent's ideas or your opponent's attack on your ideas; and finally

- conclusion.

The third rhetorical principle is **Style**. This being your own personality that you should aim to input in to your argument. All advocates need their own style – if you don't have one use CASE (Tip 30) until you develop your own.

The fourth rhetorical principle stresses the importance
of **Memory**. A good advocate should know the subject
they are to talk about well enough to be able to cope
with interruptions or challenges. However this is not
to advise you to memorise the entire speech – this is
unnecessary and unhelpful as it will make it difficult to
recover from interruptions.

Finally comes the fifth rhetorical principle which is
Delivery. This relates back to the pauses, tone of
voice, fluidity and non-verbal communication of the
advocate. Again you may wish to remind yourself of
V-STEP (Tip 34) and PIP-PEP (Tip 35) here.

There are numerous other rhetorical devices advocates should be familiar with and utilise. One is Alliteration. This is the use of different words beginning with the same sound and often the same letter.

For example, one of the most famous uses of alliteration is at the start of Abraham Lincoln's Gettysburg address:

> 'Four score and seven years ago our fathers brought forth on this continent a new nation...'

Another popular and persuasive rhetorical device is 'Antithesis'. This involves inverting the words of one proposition into a second proposition.

For example in a speech given by John F Kennedy he said:

> 'Let us never negotiate out of fear, but let us never fear to negotiate.'

'Anaphora' and 'Epiphora' are two other rhetorical devices whereby the same word is repeated either at the beginning (anaphora) or the end (epiphora) of several clauses.

An example of 'Anaphora' can be found in Dr Martin Luther King Jr's speech:

> 'I still have a dream. It is a dream deeply rooted in the American dream.
>
> I have a dream that one day this nation will rise up and live out the true meaning of its creed: 'We hold these truths to be self-evident: that all men are created equal'.
>
> I have a dream that one day on the red hills of Georgia the sons of former slaves and the sons of former slave owners will be able to sit down together at a table of brotherhood.
>
> I have a dream that one day even the state of Mississippi, a state sweltering with the heat of injustice, sweltering with the heat of oppression, will be transformed into an oasis of freedom and justice.
>
> I have a dream that my four little children will one day live in a nation where they will not be judged by the colour of their skin but by the content of their character.
>
> 'I have a dream today.'

For an example of 'Epiphora' how about this from Aaron Broussard, the then president of Jefferson Parish in the US a week after Hurricane Katrina had devastated the Gulf Coast in 2005:

> 'Take whatever idiot they have at the top of whatever agency and give me a better idiot.
>
> Give me a caring idiot.
>
> Give me a sensitive idiot.
>
> Just don't give me the same idiot.'

Advocates need to understand the fundamental
principles involved in how to argue and to grasp
that arguing is not simply contradicting what your
opponent (or the judge) has said.

You must always strive to make 'valid' arguments.
An argument is only valid if, and only if, it is not
possible that if all the premises relied upon are true the
conclusion could be false.

For example here is a valid argument referred to earlier:

Proposition 1 – Socrates is a man.

Proposition 2 – All men are mortal.

Conclusion – Therefore Socrates is Mortal.

An invalid argument would be:

Proposition 1 – Socrates is a man.

Proposition 2 – All philosophers are men.

Conclusion – Therefore Socrates is a philosopher.

The fact that an argument is invalid doesn't mean that
the argument's conclusion is itself false. The conclusion
might well be true. It's just that the invalid argument
doesn't give the decision maker any good reason to
believe that the conclusion is true.

When dealing with a valid argument if the premises
are true then the conclusion must equally be true.
Therefore an argument can be valid even if the
premises and conclusion are impossible.

For example here is a valid but unsound argument,

Proposition 1 – All cats are immortal.

Proposition 2 – Plato is a cat.

Conclusion – Plato is immortal.

Your arguments accordingly also need to be 'sound' which means, if the premises are true, and the argument is valid, then the conclusion must be true.

Therefore the first argument we looked at before (in Tip 289) is both valid and sound.

Proposition 1 – Socrates is a man.

Proposition 2 – All men are mortal.

Conclusion – Therefore Socrates is Mortal.

Whilst avoiding your own fallacious arguments, ie
arguments which are illogical, invalid and/or unsound,
you should do your utmost to point out fallacies in
your opponent's arguments.

False dilemma (aka Black and White Thinking) is an example of a fallacious argument because it is unsound:

Proposition 1 – Either claim X is true or claim Y is true,

Proposition 2 – Claim Y is false,

Conclusion – Claim X is true.

Why is this argument unsound and therefore a fallacy?

Simply because it doesn't deal with the possibility that both claims X and Y may in fact be false. The first proposition is not definitely correct.

An Appeal to Authority is another common fallacy which often occurs when experts are instructed in cases:

- Person A is an expert on subject S.

- Person A makes claim C about subject S.

- Therefore claim C is true.

It should by now be clear the various ways in which this argument is fallacious.

An important evidentiary maxim to remember is,

'False in one respect, false in all'.

Whilst this is neither a valid nor sound argument this is an example of human nature at work and how most decision makers will respond to any falsehood or distortion they may perceive you or a witness to have made.

Be aware of the Prosecutor's fallacy. This is a fallacy of statistical reasoning.

Essentially the fallacy involves assuming that the prior probability of a random match is equal to the probability that the defendant is innocent.

For example, if the perpetrator of a crime is known to have the same blood type as the defendant and only 10% of the population share the same blood type, then the prosecutor's fallacy would be to argue, on that basis alone, that the probability of the defendant being the guilty party is 90%.

Lead with your strongest point rather than building up to it. You don't know how quickly you might be interrupted!

Don't feel that you have to respond to all of your opponent's points. Focus more on tackling the strongest one or two of their points on which their argument rests.

Adopt a 'point first' style, ie state your conclusion first
to the judge then develop it.

When the judge has asked a question of your opponent and then turns to ask you the same question use the opportunity, especially if your answer is different, to advance your argument.

If possible always strive to weave your key theme, message or point into the answers to questions you are asked by the judge.

Oral argument should focus the court on the critical points and authorities. Don't rely on using pathos in the same manner as you might before a jury.

An analogy or story that fits well can enhance your argument but if there is any risk that it could be turned against you, don't use it!

More common sense advice:

'Don't get stuck on a subject – if you're in a hole get out, don't keep digging!'

Always know what it is you are asking for from the court. Some advocates address the judge without being clear on what they are actually seeking.

Remember the Rule of Three. For some reason things
that come in threes are inherently funnier, more
satisfying, effective and memorable.

An effective submission should be a dialogue but in
the form of a monologue.

The main argument needs to be obvious and should be threaded throughout your submission.

When making speeches remember Cicero's five canons of persuasion:

Introduction;

Narration;

Proof;

Refutation; and

Conclusion.

There are three tasks that need to be performed in the
Introduction:

1   warm up the audience;

2   establish a rapport with the audience; and

3   state the general claim of the argument.

Narration is where the speaker provides a summary of the relevant background information and outlines the circumstances that led to the trial.

Confirmation is where the speaker gives supporting evidence (proof) to the claim. Supporting facts and opinions from authority are included within this.

Refutation is where the opposing claims and expected objections are acknowledged, and then addressed, often by using counter-examples.

Conclusion is where the speaker then summarises the main points and reiterates the claim, sometimes ending with an appeal to pathos (ie the decision maker's emotion).

Winston Churchill had his own variation of Cicero's approach with the following template for when he drafted speeches:

A strong beginning, followed by one tight theme, simple language throughout, the use of word pictures and then an emotional ending.

A good general rule is to corroborate what you have said rather than to repeat it. Exact repetition is boring (note Tip 327) but corroboration from several angles is convincing.

An argument is more persuasive if the desired
conclusion is explicitly stated than if you leave it to the
jury to draw its own conclusions.

What gives an argument emotional impact? One aspect is 'Connection', ie something that causes the listener to feel something they equate to one of their core values.

What also produces an emotional impact is the use
of Duality or contrasts. References to Darkness and
Light, Good v Evil. Explain how good people can do
bad things or make mistakes.

A British judge Lord Neuberger has described skeleton
arguments as:

> 'the hors d'oeuvre to the main course of the
> oral submissions'

therefore if you intend filing one – keep it brief!

Avoiding clichéd phrases is obviously important as an advocate so here are a few examples of what you ought to avoid:

'At the end of the day, it is what it is.'

'Clearly . . . .'

'Obviously . . . .'

'That's the part I haven't had a chance to wrap my head around.'

'I don't disagree with you.'

'They're trying to take a second bite of the apple/cherry, aren't they?'

'But that's just a red herring, isn't it?'

'It's an exception that proves the rule!'

And always avoid mixing your metaphors:

'The long and short of it is, this is a slippery slope we're thinking of heading down.'

A cunning rhetorical device to use is 'Praeteritio' a pretended omission which actually emphasises what you're not mentioning.

For example:

> 'I don't intend to mention all the mistakes he made in the past, let us look solely at what happened on this occasion.'

An argument or issue that is not understood by
the tribunal of fact, due to a poorly structured
presentation, is more likely to be rejected.

The first advocate to argue a particular point must do
what they can within their submission to refute likely
attacks against their argument. However they should
not begin with this, nor end with it, but rather should
deal with it in the middle of what they say so that it is
not given undue emphasis.

If, in contrast, you are responding to your opponent's submission the first thing you should seek to do is to refute their argument. Doing so provides space in the listener's mind for your own submission.

Never end an argument along the lines of, 'So for all the reasons I've stated....' as this is a very feeble conclusion.

OC Jensen's assertion that:

> 'legal reasoning revolves mainly around the establishment of the minor premise'

should be understood by all advocates.

This is because the minor premise relates to the individual facts of the case. The major premise of any argument you make will come predominantly from statute and case law.

It is worth remembering that exact repetition can
bore and boredom invites intervention in some form
either with the decision maker asking you a question
or perhaps a juror daydreaming about something more
interesting.

Three questions to constantly ask yourself when deciding your arguments.

What do you want the decision maker to:

(a) know?

(b) feel?

(c) do?

Often the most persuasive precedents you can put
before a decision maker are those where the party,
similar to your client, lost at first instance but ultimately
won on appeal.

If a governing authority is against you, and you think
the decision to be wrong for some reason, such
as being outdated, you must explicitly state that.
Otherwise, on appeal, if the first instance decision
has gone against you, it may be deemed that you
previously accepted the precedent.

Sometimes you may need to refer back to discussions that occurred in the legislature to demonstrate that your interpretation of a law is the correct one.

Avoid simply giving a narrative to the decision maker
as opposed to developing a persuasive argument.
This often occurs where the advocate doesn't provide
a connection between the facts and the law.

If possible, and permissible, ensure that your
argument 'finishes in the future', ie look ahead to the
consequences if your request or submission is, or is
not, successful. What will be the impact of the decision
maker's decision?

Laying an appropriate foundation of facts is key before asking either a witness or a decision maker to go with you to the conclusion you wish them to reach.

Be aware of the 'Ladder of abstraction'. This principle is that at the top of the ladder you are dealing with something big and abstract and at the bottom you are talking about real things, specific detail. Good speeches go up and down the ladder.

Like poetry, aim to go from the particular to the universal and back again.

As far as possible try to make your argument about an individual. People are swayed far more about the plight of an individual than they are about an unknown mass.

The aim of advocacy is simple to identify – persuasion.
Persuade the decision maker to find in your favour but
what may persuade one individual may not persuade
another (remember Tip 181).

Be careful not to assert something as being true or correct simply because it hasn't yet been proven to be false.

Avoid circular arguments where the conclusion sought is buried in the premises being used to reach that conclusion.

Avoid hasty generalisations where you take one piece
of information and quickly establish a general rule or
broad principle that supports your case.

For example:

> 'This individual committed a crime of theft two
> years ago, they are now accused of theft, they
> must be a kleptomaniac.'

Never forget what all scientists know, namely that correlation does not equal causation. Just because you win lots of cases doesn't automatically mean that you are a good advocate.

USEFUL QUOTES

Quotes save you reinventing the wheel – whatever you want to say may already have been said by someone else in a far simpler and more effective way so again we return to CASE (Tip 30).

One example for when the opposing advocate says that something is 'obvious' is the following quote from Sir Arthur Conan Doyle, the creator of Sherlock Holmes:

> 'There is nothing more deceptive than an obvious fact.'

A quote for when you are dealing with cases to do with your client engaging in potentially risky or reckless behaviour:

'Risks must be taken, because the greatest hazard in life is to risk nothing.'

Leo Buscaglia

In a case where you've shown an opposing witness to
be a liar about something you could try the following
(but only where humour won't cause you any harm
and the judge won't be offended!):

> 'Credibility is very much like virginity. Once
> you lose it, it's impossible to regain.'

Israel Scoble

Where your witness has missed something, that the
decision maker might expect them to have been
aware of, the following quote from Johann Wolfgang
van Goethe may assist:

'The hardest thing to see is what is in front of
your eyes.'

When a witness's intention is a crucial issue another quote from Goethe can be useful:

'If you wish to know the mind of a man, listen to his words'.

If you need to attack statistics that your opponent is quoting the following may prove of assistance:

'Statistics are human beings with the tears dried off'

Paul Brodeur

Should your opponent rely on the decision maker's
'common sense' you can often be at a disadvantage so if
appropriate try this quote from Albert Einstein:

> 'Common sense is the collection of prejudices
> acquired by age 18.'

Where a witness for the opposing party has omitted to
say something emphasise the point with the following
quote from Martin Luther:

'You are not only responsible for what you say,
but also for what you do not say.'

When your opponent or a witness has been loud or aggressive in their approach you may wish to undermine their vociferousness with the following,

'Where there is shouting, there is no true knowledge.'

Leonardo da Vinci

A quote for both yourself to apply and to perhaps use against a loquacious opponent:

'Do not say a little in many words, but a great deal in few'

Pythagoras

A quote for when an opposing party or witness says that they 'wished' that they had done something other than what they had actually done:

> 'Never grow a wishbone where your backbone ought to be.'

Dorothy Parker

Should your case involve examining the individual actions of a large, important organisation, in contrast to the action of your client, who is a single individual, the following quote from Honore de Balzac may be of assistance:

'Laws are spider webs through which the big flies pass and the little ones get caught'.

RESOURCES TO IMPROVE YOUR ADVOCACY

One way to improve your advocacy is to get a mentor, ie is a more experienced advocate, with whom you can discuss ideas and receive constructive feedback.

Whenever you ask for feedback from someone, whether it be another advocate, judge or friend, simply listen to their subjective view. Don't seek to explain, justify or undermine their response. Instead say, 'Thank you, that's really helpful' and go away and reflect on what they have said. The likelihood is that they will undoubtedly be willing to give you more feedback and even more honest feedback in the future.

What do you think is likely to happen if you respond negatively to their feedback?

Want to improve your advocacy over the internet? Coursera.org provide a number of free programmes on rhetoric, how to argue, and improving your writing all of which can improve aspects of your advocacy.

Strive to learn from your mistakes and a text to read to help you to do so is *Mistakes were made, but not by me*, Tavris and Aronson (Pinter & Martin Ltd, 2013)

For a telling analysis of what jurors actually think about the advocates who appear in front of them read the findings of US District Court Judge James W. Hoolihan at: http://mnbenchbar.com/2014/02/what-jurors-think-about-attorneys/

An essential free resource for all professionals involved in criminal justice is theadvocatesgateway. org.

This website gathers together best practice guidance and advice in relation to the questioning of vulnerable witnesses of all descriptions whether due to their age, learning difficulties, mental health or similar issues.

To learn just how bad human beings are at recognising other people read Professor Vicky Bruce's book, *Face Perception* (Psychology Press, 2011)

Influence by Robert Cialdini (1st edn, Harper Business, 2007) is an interesting and valuable read on the make up of persuasion.

Another helpful book to read is one written by Claudia Hammond, *Time Warped: Unlocking the Mysteries of Time Perception* (Canongate Books, 2013).

This text explains how people perceive time and crucially the factors that influence this. It is incredibly helpful when dealing with cases where timings may be a key determining factor in the decision.

To learn and understand fallacious arguments
read the free ebook by Dr Michael C Labossiere,
42 Fallacies.

Another book recommendation:

Daniel Kahneman's, *Thinking, Fast and Slow* (Penguin, 2012) is an essential read for all advocates on the process of decision making.

Read it to learn what leads decision makers to make the decisions they do.

As well as the law advocates need to know about psychology since the law is generally related to human behaviour and interaction.

A useful primer that has tips on lots of relevant psychological phenomena that all advocates would benefit from reading is Daniel Simons and Christopher Chabris', *The Invisible Gorilla* (Reprint edition, Harmony, 2011).